ACKNOWLEDGMENTS

I wish to thank the many people I wore out in sometimes lively discussions concerning the role of women in marriage and the life and leadership of the Church.

You know who you are.

We did not always agree, but I still gained something useful from our conversations.

TABLE OF CONTENTS

A NOTE FROM THE AUTHOR

I am a life-long student of the Bible. I love it and believe it to be God's perfect written Word.

While I study to understand the scriptures better, I aspire even more to be a faithful disciple of the Living Word - the Lord Jesus Christ.

If you are looking for a scholarly work, this is not it. I know scholars who can exegete the hair off a mosquito at one hundred paces. I am not writing for scholars, but the rest of us.

I believe in the inerrancy of the Bible as written in its original languages. Sadly, the translation process and cultural biases have occasionally clouded the meaning of the original text.

Sometimes the words we use mean one thing in the original language, but something entirely different in English.

One of the problematic Greek words is "kephale" (kef-al-AY) [Strong's NT 2776].

Kephale means "head."

Most of the time, kephale refers to the thing sitting on top of our necks; but in a handful of uses, it means something else. That's where we find the problem.

If I were to tell you I am the head of a company, what would that mean to you?

To most English speakers, it means I'm the boss, but not to a Greek living two thousand years ago.

To a Greek living at the time the New Testament was written, head did not mean boss; it meant "source."

This difference in meaning has spawned enormous consequences. The inadvertently changed meaning of certain scriptures in English has caused considerable, multi-generational harm to millions of Christ's followers.

This study will restore the original meaning of the affected verses, so we can understand what God is actually saying to us.

> *Acts 17:11 For they received the word with great eagerness, examining the scriptures daily to see whether these things were so.*

The Apostle Paul commended the Berean people for testing the teachings they received. I invite you to do the same.

I pray this study will aid you in your search for truth, and that you will find, if you have not already, the One who is the Truth.

Housekeeping

Throughout this book, I will compare verses as traditionally rendered with a revised version. I will also explain why the revisions are necessary.

I am <u>not</u> rewriting the scriptures. My goal is to render each verse as near to the meaning of the original text as possible.

I have rendered these verses as people living at the time they were written would have understood them.

The Bible is supposed to mean the same thing to people living today as it did to people living centuries ago. By eliminating modern cultural biases, their original meaning is clarified and restored.

In all revised scriptures presented in this study, words not found in the Greek text are shown in parentheses.

WHERE "HEAD" WAS ADDED

First, let us look at verses where head was added to the English text, even though it is absent from the Greek text. We find these additions in 1st Corinthians 11:6 and 11:13.

In 1st Corinthians 11:3, head was added three times:

> **Traditional:** *For if a woman does not cover her **head**, let her also have her hair cut off; but if it is disgraceful for a woman to have her hair cut off or her **head** shaved, let her cover her **head**.*

> **Revised:** *For if (a) woman (is) not covered, let her also be shorn; but if (it is) disgraceful for a woman to be shorn or shaven, let her be covered.*

In 1st Corinthians 11:13, we find the fourth and final instance where the word head was added:

> **Traditional** *Judge for yourselves: is it proper for a woman to pray to God with her **head** uncovered?*

> **Revised**: *Judge for yourselves: is it proper (for) a woman (to) pray to God uncovered?*

Adding head to the text in both these verses does not alter the intended meaning. It aids our understanding.

GREEK WORDS THAT MEAN "HEAD"

The English version of the New Testament translates three different Greek words to mean head. There are no issues with most of them. The problems occur only a handful of times.

The three words translated head are:

- ❖ Stachus (STAHK'-oos) [Strong's NT 4719]
- ❖ Oikodespotes (oy-kod-es-POT-ace) [Strong's NT 3617]
- ❖ Kephale (kef-al-AY) [Strong's NT 2776]

Stachus

Stachus means "a head or ear of grain." We find it in Matthew 12:1, Mark 2:23, Mark 4:28 (twice), and Luke 6:1.

I will give just one example found in Mark 4:2. You can explore the other verses on your own:

Traditional: The soil produces crops by itself; first the blade, then the **head**, then the mature grain in the **head**.

Revised: The soil produces crops by itself; first (the) blade, then (the) **ear**, then after that (the) mature grain in the **ear.**

There's no issue here; replacing ear with head doesn't alter the meaning of the passage.

Oikodespotes

Oikodespotes means "ruler of the house(hold)." Our English word "despot," meaning "tyrant," is derived from despotes.

We find oikosdespotes in Matthew 10:25, 13:27, 13:52, 20:1, 20:11, 21:33, 24:43, Mark 14:14, Luke 12:39, 13:25, 14:21, and 22:11.

Let us look at Matthew 10:25:

*Traditional: It is enough for the disciple that he become like his teacher and the slave like his master. If they have called the **head of the house** Satan, how much more will they malign the members of his household?*

> **Revised:** *It is enough for the disciple that they become like their teacher and the slave like their master. If they have called the **ruler of the household** Satan, how much more (will they malign) the members of his household?*

All the pronouns in this verse are gender-neutral, including the one traditionally translated "his."

Jesus draws us a picture here; in this story,

He is the ruler of the household. He is the one being called Satan.

Jesus shows us if people are willing to mock, slander, and attempt to discredit Him by comparing Him to Satan, then His followers can expect the same or worse abuse.

Matthew 13:52:

> **Traditional:** *And Jesus said to them, "Therefore, every scribe who has become a disciple of the Kingdom of Heaven is like a **head of a household**, who brings out of his treasure things new and old."*

> **Revised:** *Then He said to them, "Therefore, every scribe who has become a disciple of the Kingdom of Heaven is like someone, a **ruler of a household**, who brings out of their treasure (things) new and old."*

In every verse where we find oikodespotes, the pronouns referring to the ruler of the household are gender-neutral. The ruler of the household may be a man or a woman.

Matthew 13:27:

> **Traditional:** *The slaves of the **landowner** came and said to him, 'Sir, did you not sow good seed in your field? How then does it have tares?'*
>
> **Revised:** *The slaves of the **ruler of the household** came and said to him, 'Sir, did you not sow good seed in your field? How then does it have weeds?"*

A "kurios" is a person with supreme authority. It is translated here as "sir." In this verse, the slaves address the ruler of the household as sir - an honorific typically addressed to a man.

One reference describing the ruler of the household as a man does not require us to conclude that all rulers of the household must be men.

Kephale

Now we come to the word whose translation has caused many problems. "Kephale" appears in the New Testament seventy-five times.

Kephale – as the Head on Top of Our Necks

Fifty-eight of those seventy-five times, kephale means the head on top of our necks.

These are the scriptures where kephale means our physical heads:

> Matthew 5:36, 6:17, 8:20, 10:30, 14:8, 14:11, 26:7, 27:29, 27:30, & 27:37
> Mark 6:24, 6:25, 6:27, 6:28, 12:4, 14:3, & 15:19
> Luke 7:38, 7:46, 9:58, 12:7, & 21:18
> John 13:9, 19:2, 20:7, & 20:12
> Acts 27:34, Romans 12:20
> 1st Corinthians 11:4, 11:5 (twice), 11:6 (three times), 11:7, 11:10, & 12:21
> Revelation 1:14, 10:1, 12:1, 14:14, & 19:12

None of these references are at issue.

Kephale – as the Cornerstone

Now we shall examine five verses where kephale is used in conjunction with the Greek word "gonia," which means "corner."

The meaning is "head of the corner," or "cornerstone."

The scriptures are:

Matthew 21:42, Mark 12:10, Luke 20:17, Acts 4:11, and 1st Peter 2:7.

All five verses quote Psalm 118:22:

*The stone which the builders rejected has become the chief **cornerstone**.*

We will examine one example. You can explore the other verses on your own:

Matthew 21:42:

> *Jesus said to them, "Did you never read in the Scriptures;*
> *'The stone which the builders rejected,*
> *This became the chief **cornerstone**;*
> *This came about from the Lord,*
> *And it is marvelous in our eyes?'"*

A cornerstone is the first and most important stone in the building of a foundation. It guides the construction of the rest of the building.

A properly-placed cornerstone ensures the stability of the entire structure.

Place it with care, and the building will stand. Place it carelessly, and the building will fall.

We cannot overemphasize the importance of a strong cornerstone.

Matthew 21:42 tells us Jesus is the cornerstone of our faith, the fulfillment of Psalm 118:22:

- ❖ The Jewish spiritual leaders of His day rejected their Messiah.
- ❖ Jesus is the foundation of the Christian faith.
- ❖ The tremendous power of God brought this to pass.

Jesus is the source of our strength and stability. He is the cornerstone of His Church.

Kephale - as Source

The remaining twelve uses of kephale are problematic.

It is technically correct to translate kephale to mean head in these verses.

However, because head means boss or ruler to a modern-day English speaker, translators should use source in its place.

Doing so eliminates the cultural bias that changes the original meaning of the scriptures where kephale appears.

Unfortunately, that has not happened. Because source did not replace head, a lack of clarity, absent in the original languages, is found in modern English translations of the scriptures.

This lack of clarity has been a source of centuries of needless confusion, pain, and suffering within the Body of Christ, giving rise to harmful false doctrines.

It has produced doctrines that reduce the one-flesh nature of marriage to a master-slave relationship and relegate women to second-class citizenship in the life and leadership of the Church.

These are the verses where this cultural bias has altered their meaning:

> 1st Corinthians 11:3 (3 times), 11:4, & 11:5
> Ephesians 1:22, 4:15, & 5:23 (twice)
> Colossians 1:18, 2:10, & 2:19

The Greeks did not know the human head (the brain) was the ruling member of the body. They believed the head was the source of life.

They knew if you cut off an arm or a leg, you would probably die, but you might live. However, if you cut off the head, you died 100% of the time!

While the Greeks believed the head served no additional purpose for a woman, it performed a second important function for a man.

A man's head contained another source of life - sperm.

The Greeks believed sperm traveled from the man's head, down the spinal cord, and into the woman during intercourse, where it planted itself in the womb.

They did not know about the fertilization or existence of the egg. The Greeks believed, if you could examine sperm closely enough, you would find a tiny human being complete in every detail.

The Greeks believed women contributed nothing to the conception of a child. The womb was merely the soil where a baby took root and grew.

HEAD TO THE SOURCE

There is another interesting bit of evidence to support the translation of kephale as source. The Greeks customarily placed a bust of a bull or a human male at the source of their rivers.

The description of this custom survives in an English word; "headwater."

A headwater is the source or beginning of a river.

CHRISTIAN ORDER? OR SOMETHING ELSE?

Many scholars believe the first sixteen verses of 1ˢᵗ Corinthians 11 are among the most difficult to understand. I studied them intensely for years before I felt competent to teach about them.

In this study, I am only going to cover the verses that are relevant to the discussion of the meaning of the word head.

A Misleading Headline

The heading before 1ˢᵗ Corinthians 11 usually reads something like "Christian Order." However, Paul addresses several other topics before he finally gets to the subject of disorderly behavior in verse 17.

While the scriptures are trustworthy in their original languages, the headings, added centuries later, are not always reliable.

The heading before 1ˢᵗ Corinthians 11 is one of them.

It distorts and obscures the meaning of the scriptures that follow it.

A more accurate headline might read: "Jesus is God, Come in the Flesh."

A Misunderstood Text

We want to understand better what the Apostle Paul is teaching the church at Corinth in 1st Corinthians 11:2-3. Let's start with verse two:

> *Now I praise you because you remember me in everything and hold firmly to the traditions, just as I delivered them to you.*

All religions have laws and traditions.

Here, Paul commends the Corinthian church for following the laws and traditions he taught them.

If we desire to follow God, obeying religious laws and traditions is an excellent place to start, but that is where all religions begin and end.

Except for Christianity.

There is much more to Christianity than laws, rituals, and traditions.

In verse three, Paul writes to show us what makes the Christian faith, unlike every other religion on earth:

> *Traditional: But I want you to understand that Christ is the **head** of every man, and the man is the **head** of a woman, and God is the **head** of Christ.*

Given western culture's tendency to interpret head to mean boss or ruler, a casual reading of verse three seems to indicate Paul is showing us a power structure.

It seems to show that Christ is the ruler of all men, and men, in turn, are the rulers of women. Finally, God (presumably the Father) is revealed as the ruler of Christ.

Teachers and preachers often explain the reference to Christ at the top and bottom of the power structure by saying that He is the Alpha and Omega.

Therefore, we find Him at the beginning, and again at the end of the power structure.

But if kephale is rendered correctly as source, the power structure disappears, as it should:

> *Revised: But I want you to understand that Christ is the **source** of every man, and the man is the **source** of a woman, and God is the **source** of Christ.*

This verse does <u>not</u> describe a power structure.

It presents a <u>timeline</u>.

Paul is writing to prove that Jesus is God, come in the flesh!

Obeying the law and following the traditions of our faith is good, but it cannot save us.

Only Jesus can save us. Only Jesus can make us whole.

That God became flesh, lived among us, sacrificed His life to pay the penalty for our sin, and rose from the dead so that we might live too is what makes the Christian faith unique!

Rightly Dividing Verse Three

Verse three does not establish a power structure in the Church, as many believe.

It shows us a timeline that proves Jesus' divinity and humanity.

There are four points in the timeline:

First Point: The Pre-Incarnate Christ

> *But I want you to understand that Christ is the **source** of every man*

The first point in the timeline shows us Jesus Christ is eternal; He existed <u>before</u> He was born into this world as a human baby.

It is through Jesus and by Jesus that all things were created and exist. Jesus is the source of every man.

Second Point: Adam, the First Human Being

> *…Christ is the **source** of every man and the man*

The pronouns concerning the second point in the timeline are masculine because Paul used "andros," a word that generally refers only to males.

Adam is the first human being Christ created.

Christ is the Creator and Source of all persons, both male and female. All human beings, with only one exception, are descended from Adam.

Jesus is the exception. A virgin conceived and gave birth to Him by the power of the Holy Spirit.

When we see the phrase "the man" in the scriptures, it is usually a reference to Adam.

God created Adam from the dust of the earth and breathed life into him. Adam became a living soul.

Third Point: Eve, the Second Human Being

> *…and the man is the **source** of a woman,*

This part of the verse revealing the third point of our timeline does not refer to women in general, but a specific woman - Eve.

God decided it was not good for Adam to be alone, so He put him to sleep, took a rib from his side, and used Adam's flesh, blood, and bone to create Eve, his female ally, and counterpart.

Christ created both Adam and Eve; only the material He used differed. He made Adam from dust, but Eve came from Adam's side.

If Eve had also been created from dust, her full humanity might have been questioned.

That Eve came from Adam's side leaves no room to doubt her full humanity, nor her full equality with Adam.

That Adam is Eve's source, does not contradict the truth that God is their Creator, and the primary source of life for them both.

Temporal Primacy: The false doctrine of "temporal primacy" postulates that women are inferior to men and must be ruled by them because God made Adam first.

Nonsense.

If we extend this doctrine to its logical and fullest extent, then Adam must be placed under the authority of all animals, because God created them before He created Adam!

Sin Brought Inequality and Slavery: When sin and death cut the bond of intimacy between Adam and Eve, and between them and their Creator (the primary source of their lives), they both became slaves to the secondary source of their lives:

- ❖ Adam came from the ground and became a slave to the ground.
- ❖ Eve came from the side of Adam and became a slave to Adam.

Women did not become the slaves and property of men because it was the will and plan of God from the beginning.

It came about because sin and death came into the world and took away humankind's freedom!

Jesus' death and resurrection set men free from their slavery to the ground and set women free from their bondage to men - though it seems to be taking a long time for some among us to figure that out and walk in it!

Jesus destroyed the power of sin and death, and in the process, restored the original equality of men and women.

He restored Eve's ministry as Adam's equal partner, ally, and sometimes, rescuer.

There should be no second-class citizens in the Kingdom of God. May the whole Church take hold of this truth at last!

Fourth Point: Jesus Christ Incarnate

> *…and God is the **source** of Christ.*

The final point in the timeline reveals the fulfillment of God's promise - that His Son would someday undo the damage done in the Garden when humankind fell into sin.

Jesus is the only human being who is not "of the seed" of Adam. He did not have a human father.

His mother, the Virgin Mary, was found to be with child by the power of the Holy Spirit.

When Mary gave birth to the sinless Son of God, the stage was set for the fulfillment of the prophetic word God spoke to Satan:

> *Genesis 3:15 "And I will put enmity between you and the woman, and between your seed and her Seed; He shall bruise you on the head, and you shall bruise Him on the heel."*

Genesis 3:15 promised that the Seed of Eve (Jesus Christ, the sacrificial Lamb of God) would destroy Satan and all his evil works.

When Jesus bruised Satan on the head, He destroyed the source of Satan's works. The best Satan could do in return was wound the Savior.

The wounds Christ suffered heal us. The worst damage Satan could do to our Lord has become healing for the Bride of Christ!

Since the cross, Satan has been rendered powerless by Jesus Christ.

He retains his control of unbelievers, but the only power Satan has over followers of Christ is the power we give him.

He is nothing more than God's unwilling servant!

Here again, are the four points in the timeline:

- ❖ Pre-incarnate Christ.
- ❖ Creation of Adam.
- ❖ Creation of Eve.
- ❖ Birth of Christ Incarnate – our Savior.

Christianity is not merely about laws and traditions. It is about a person - Jesus Christ.

Obeying the law and following the traditions of our faith is good, but it cannot save us. Only Jesus can save us. Only Jesus can make us whole.

Paul did not establish or describe a power structure when he wrote 1st Corinthians 11:2-3; he wrote it to prove Jesus is God!

That God became flesh, lived among us, sacrificed His life to pay the penalty for our sin, and rose from the dead so that we might live too is what makes the Christian faith unique!

Let us rightly divide the scriptures, so we might see and understand the plan and purpose of God.

GIVE NO OFFENSE

After Paul praised the Corinthian church in verse two for following the laws and traditions he had taught them, he revealed in verse three what makes Christianity unique.

In verse four, Paul returned to the subject of tradition, teaching the church in Corinth the same thing my wife and I taught our children - to be sensitive to the customs, traditions, and taboos of others. By so doing, they might earn the opportunity to share the gospel.

The scriptures tell us followers of Christ are no longer subject to the Law of Moses. We are the beneficiaries of a new covenant, free to be led by the Holy Spirit.

While we enjoy tremendous freedom in Christ, the Lord may sometimes ask us to give up our freedom so that those around us might meet and come to know the Living God.

Verses 4-6 tell us to be sensitive to the customs of others, so we do not offend them and thereby lose an opportunity to share the gospel:

> ***Traditional:*** *1st Corinthians 11:4 Every man who has something on his **head** while praying or prophesying disgraces his **head**.*

> ***Revised:*** *Every man praying or prophesying (while) having his **head** covered dishonors his **source**.*

The traditional English understanding of the meaning of head would lead us to believe the man who prays while wearing a hat disgraces his boss.

The revised version shows us it is not a man's boss, but his source that he disgraces.

Who is every man's source? As we have seen, Jesus Christ is our source.

How does it dishonor Jesus for a man to pray while wearing a hat?

In those days, men who meticulously followed the laws and traditions of their faith prayed with their heads covered. A man wore a hat to cover his sin symbolically so that he could approach a holy deity in prayer. Many religions still observe this custom in many parts of the world.

If we follow Him, the blood of Jesus has covered our sin and set us free from sin. Wearing a hat while we pray is no longer required.

In the days when Paul was writing to the church at Corinth, if a Christian man wore a head covering while he prayed, observers might conclude Jesus' sacrifice on the cross was not enough to save the wearer from his sin.

Therefore, if a male believer wore a head covering while praying, doing so could dishonor Christ, his source, in the eyes of observers.

To avoid this misunderstanding, Paul instructed men to pray with their heads uncovered, as an outward sign that Jesus' sacrifice was enough to save us from our sin.

Today, men still remove their hats while praying, as a sign of respect for the Lord.

A STRICTER STANDARD FOR WOMEN?

After instructing men concerning prayer, he next instructed women.

A quick reading of 1st Corinthians 11:5 might lead us to believe Paul has established one set of rules for men when they pray, and a different standard for women.

Not so.

> **Traditional:** *But every woman who has her **head** uncovered while praying or prophesying disgraces her **head**, for she is one and the same as the woman whose **head** is shaved.*

> **Revised:** *But every woman who has her **head** uncovered while praying or prophesying disgraces her **source**, for she is one and the same as the woman whose **head** is shaved.*

Greek women who followed Jesus had two sources. The first was Jesus. The second was her husband.

That her husband was her source is an illustration of the biblical truth that Eve came from the side of Adam.

If a woman prayed with her head uncovered, it disgraced her husband, and through him, Jesus Christ.

If we want to understand why an uncovered woman disgraced her source when she prayed, it is essential to know what Greek women wore, and why.

Welcome to Las Corinth

Corinth was an important seaport at the time of Paul's writing. Like most seaports, it was a cosmopolitan melting pot, where people of many nations mingled. It was also a city skilled at separating sailors from their money.

The Las Vegas of the Mediterranean world, Corinth, was famous for its prostitutes and immorality.

"To live like a Corinthian" was a Mediterranean saying that needed no explanation.

Historians estimate the government of Corinth alone employed as many as 1,500 prostitutes. Their activities generated significant revenue for the city.

A sailor stepping off a ship in Corinth could tell at a glance whether he could approach a woman for sex.

There were four kinds of women in ancient Greece:

Wives: Wives dressed modestly. They wore a head covering, a veil, and a floor-length dress, though their arms might be bare.

Wives did not leave the house very often. They had escorts when they did.

Wives were their husbands' property; our lonely sailor could not approach them.

Concubines: These were the Greek equivalent of Japanese geishas. They wore a head covering, but no veil. Their hair might be visible and elaborately styled.

Their dress was the best money could buy and fashionable. Concubines wore makeup and expensive jewelry.

Concubines would also have escorts. They were the property of the men who kept them.

Our sailor was out of luck as far as they were concerned.

Common Prostitutes: The prostitutes who worked for themselves, a pimp, or the city did not wear a head covering. Their hair might be braided or loose and flowing.

The richness of their dress depended on how prosperous they were.

Our sailor friend could approach them.

Temple Prostitutes: These also did not wear a head covering. Their heads were bald, a sign they served one of the gods.

Having sex with them could be considered an act of worship of the god they represented. Our sailor friend could approach them, as well.

Prostitution was common in Greece but was still considered a shameful occupation. Any wife who went out in public without wearing a head covering might be mistaken for a prostitute, and thereby bring disgrace to her husband (her source).

Paul wanted Christian women to wear a head covering when and where the culture required it. He was not interested in setting up a stricter standard of behavior for women; he did it to promote the gospel.

Christians can establish relationships and earn the right to share the gospel if we avoid offending people.

The gospel is offensive enough to many. We ought not to allow our actions or attitudes to add to the offense.

Conforming to cultural norms helps bring down barriers to the gospel, provided we don't violate our consciences or abandon our moral standards.

By giving up our freedom when circumstances require it, we can better offer Jesus' love and demonstrate the character of Christ to a hurting and doubting world.

In many nations today, tradition, law, and religion require women to be veiled and covered in public.

In theory, women who wear a head covering and veil are thought to be respectable and can safely venture out in public without being harassed or attacked.

On the other hand, men can, and often do, insult and abuse women who fail to cover themselves.

Cultures that require adult females to wear the veil blame women, when their beauty and sexuality tempt men.

Therefore, since men cannot control their urges and refuse to wear blindfolds, women must cover up!

THE HUSBAND IS THE HEAD OF THE WIFE

Ephesians 5:23:

> ***Traditional:*** *For the husband is the **head** of the wife, as Christ also is the **head** of the church, He Himself being the Savior of the Body.*
>
> ***Revised:*** *For (the) husband is the **source** of (the) wife, as even the Christ (is the) **source** of the Church; (and) He (is the) Savior of the Body.*

If there is any place in the scriptures where the difference between the English and Greek meaning of head has caused confusion and pain when it should have brought life and peace, it is Ephesians 5:23.

Women have long suffered as the slaves and property of men when they ought to have been free and equal.

There are no second-class citizens in the Kingdom of God.

Most Christians agree marriage between a man and a woman is a representation or foreshadowing of the coming union between Christ and His Bride. We find that point of view illustrated in Ephesians.

Paul takes us back to the first marriage. Eve represents the Bride of Christ; Adam represents Christ.

Eve came from the side of Adam, thus making Adam her source.

Here is the parallel:

- ❖ A wound was made in Adam's side, and his blood was shed to bring forth his bride.
- ❖ A wound was made in Jesus' side, and His blood was shed to bring forth His Bride.

As Jesus hung on the cross, a Roman soldier stuck a spear in His side to make sure He was dead. The scriptures tell us water and blood poured forth from the wound.

The shed blood of Christ saves us. We are baptized in the water of regeneration.

Paul then reminds us that Jesus alone is the Savior of His Body. No human husband has that power. No human effort can save us.

We are all, whether male or female, dependent upon the Lord for all things, but especially for life itself.

IS JESUS THE RULER OF THE CHURCH?

There is another reason we can be confident source is the correct meaning of head. At the time Paul wrote, and at this moment in history, Jesus is not yet the ruler of the Church.

> *Matthew 20:25-28 But Jesus called them (to Himself and) said, "You know that the rulers of the Gentiles subjugate them, and they that are great exercise authority over them.*
>
> *"But it shall not be so among you; therefore, whoever wishes (to) be great among you shall be your servant,*
>
> *"And whoever wishes (to) be first among you shall be your slave;*
>
> *"Just as the Son of Man came, not to be served, but to serve, and to give His life (as) a ransom for many."*

Jesus contrasts worldly and spiritual power in these verses.

In the world, strong leaders dominate and exploit the weak; but in the Church, the strong are supposed to serve the vulnerable.

Jesus did not come to be the kind of ruler the Jewish people expected, a leader who would kick the Romans out of the Holy Land and establish a Jewish kingdom.

He came to be a servant.

Jesus demonstrated His perfect love for us when He did something no one expected. He surrendered Himself to the most brutal torture and death that could be devised by the sadistic imagination of fallen humankind.

For love's sake, He gave up the most precious thing any human being has; life itself. Jesus Christ, the ultimate servant, made Himself a slave!

After His resurrection, Jesus left to prepare a place for His Bride. Meanwhile, His Bride, with the help of the Holy Spirit, prepares herself for the return of her Beloved.

Jesus rules in our lives today, not because He has claimed His divine and lawful right to do so; but because we who love Him have responded to His sacrificial and perfect love with the surrender of our hearts and lives to Him.

However, we also know Jesus is coming again. When He returns, He will come as a King!

Philippians 2:10-11 That at the name of Jesus every knee will bow, (of those who are in) Heaven, and on earth, and under the earth,

And every tongue will confess that Jesus Christ is Lord, to the glory of God (the) Father.

JESUS: SOURCE (HEAD) OF THE CHURCH

We have seen that Jesus is the source of the Church, but not yet the ruler of the Church.

He rules in our hearts because, in response to His love, we have surrendered ourselves to Him.

We also know He will return on a day only the Father knows.

He will come not only to rule the Church but to assume His throne as the King of all Creation.

When that day comes, it will not matter whether people love Him or believe in Him or not. Everyone in heaven, on the earth, and under the earth shall witness His power and majesty.

All flesh will bow down in the dust before Him and declare Him Lord.

JESUS HAS PREEMINENCE

Paul's description of Christ as the source of the Church can also be found in Colossians 1:18:

> ***Traditional:*** *He is also **head** of the body, the church; and He is the beginning, the firstborn from the dead so that He Himself will come to have first place in everything.*

> ***Revised:*** *And He is the **source** of the body, the church, who is (the) beginning, firstborn from the dead, that He might have complete preeminence.*

We already know Jesus is the source of His Body, the Church. He is the Alpha and Omega, the beginning and end, the One who has always lived, lives today, and lives forever.

Jesus is also the first human being to be permanently raised from the dead.

The Bible tells us Jesus raised Lazarus from the dead, but even though the scriptures do not record it, we can be sure he died a second time. Lazarus no longer lives among us on the earth.

But Jesus rose from the dead, walked around for a while in the same body He had before His crucifixion, then returned to Heaven. He is still alive today. He lives in us, and we live in Him. It is true; apart from Him, we can do nothing.

Because Jesus is the first to be permanently raised from the dead, He has temporal preeminence; that is, His permanent resurrection from the dead was the first in history. We are raised from the dead because He rose from the dead. We live because He lives.

To have preeminence sometimes means to be first in rank, to be the chief ruler of a hierarchy or power structure.

However, as we have already seen, Jesus' return as King will take place sometime in the future.

If we want to understand what Paul is saying to us, we must adopt another meaning for preeminence; to be first in influence.

To be first in influence means Jesus uses the gentle persuasion of love, rather than brute force, to invite us to follow Him. Gentle persuasion perfectly describes the way Jesus leads His Church today.

Jesus is not like a western shepherd, who drives the sheep ahead of him using force, fear, and a well-trained sheepdog.

He is an eastern shepherd, the Good Shepherd, who cares for the sheep, going before them and calling them by name to follow Him.

Jesus is the door of the sheep. He lies down in the opening to the sheepfold at night to protect His flock. He puts His life on the line for the sake of His sheep.

The wolf cannot attack the flock without first facing and defeating the shepherd. Satan tried; Jesus defeated him.

> *John 10:27 My sheep hear my voice, and I know them, and they follow me.*

Jesus is our Good Shepherd. We follow Him, not out of fear or compulsion, but because we hear Him, know His voice, and love Him.

Rather than establish Jesus' rank in a power structure, this verse reveals His complete sufficiency as our source.

We can rely on Him for everything we need.

POWER STRUCTURES: A POOR SUBSTITUTE FOR LOVE

We tend to seek safety and security in power and power structures when we can only find it in Christ's love.

The traditional translation of Ephesians 1:22 shows us an example of this tendency:

> **Traditional:** *And He put all things in subjection under His feet, and gave Him as* **head** *over all things to the church,*

> **Revised:** *And all (things) He put under His feet and gave Him as the* **source** *of all (things) to the church,*

Notice that the phrase "in subjection" is missing from the revised text. That is because it does not appear in the original text.

This phrase concerning subjection invented and arbitrarily inserted in the passage, neither advances nor clarifies the meaning of the text. Worse, it leads us away from the intent of the Author. It should not have been added.

The Greeks believed the "Fates" ruled the destinies of all humankind; there was no way to escape their control.

The Apostle Paul disagreed. He wrote to comfort us, telling us God the Father has placed all principalities and powers – all things – under Jesus' feet.

Nothing in God's creation rises to the level of equality with Jesus. All things fall short of His perfection, and therefore, are under His feet.

But they are not beneath His notice.

His love is pure and utterly complete. We are under Jesus' protection and, therefore, secure.

Paul reminds us that Jesus Christ (not the Fates, or anything or anyone else) is the sole source of all things for those who are part of His Church.

We see this thought completed in Ephesians 1:23:

> *…which is His Body, the fullness of Him who fills all in all.*

The Church is both the Bride and the Body of Christ.

As the head of His Body, Jesus is the source of all things for everyone who knows Him as Lord and Savior. He is a complete and sufficient source of everything we need.

He is complete, and we are made complete in Him.

THE UNITY OF CHRIST'S BODY

In Ephesians, the Apostle Paul wrote about the world-wide unity of the Church, the Body of Christ.

It is not a mere organizational unity, a power structure maintained by human effort or will. It is an organic, active, living union with Jesus Christ. It is a pre-existing unity, flowing from Jesus Christ, our source.

Ephesians 4:15:

> **Traditional:** *But speaking the truth in love, we are to grow up in all aspects into Him who is the **head**, even Christ,*

> **Revised:** *But speaking the truth with love, (we) are (to) grow up (in) all (aspects) into Him who is the **source**; Christ,*

Again, we do not have to work to bring about unity in the Church. Church unity cannot be established or maintained by mere human effort.

Rather than labor for an unreachable goal, the Lord invites us to enter the <u>already existing</u> unity of the Body of Christ, established through Jesus and maintained by the Holy Spirit.

Our mission is to go out into the world (as opposed to huddling in our church buildings, angry at, fearful of, and judging the world) and make disciples.

Our joy is greatly enhanced as we become familiar with the scriptures, learn how to be led by the Holy Spirit, and contribute to the health of the Body by using our God-given gifts for His glory.

By so doing, we become mature in our faith:

> **Revised:** *Ephesians 4:14-15 That (from now on, we) will no longer (be) children, tossed here and there (by waves), and carried about by every wind of doctrine, by the trickery of men, by craftiness in deceitful scheming;*
>
> *But speaking the truth with love, (we) are (to) grow up (in) all (aspects) into Him who is the* **source***; Christ.*

Again, when we replace the English meaning of head as ruler with the Greek meaning of head as source, we come much closer to the intent of the Author.

God does not invite us to become insignificant cogs in a vast power structure controlled by those above us.

Instead, He invites us to become mature and fully-participating members of His Body, whose life flows from the source, Jesus Christ.

JESUS: SOURCE OF ALL POWER AND AUTHORITY

Our insistence on looking for power structures when we ought to be looking for love comes to the forefront in this typical translation of Colossians 2:10:

> **Traditional:** *And in Him, you have been made complete, and He is the **head** over all rule and authority.*

> **Revised:** *And you are complete in Him, who is the **source** of all rule and authority;*

In keeping with our obsession with power structures, we invent laws, rules, and regulations. Human leaders (often self-appointed) then take it upon themselves to judge those who fail to obey.

The usurpation of God's judgment seat has a long, sorry history.

In our legalism, we allow our rules and traditions to become more important to us than friendship with Christ. We forge chains to bind and separate us from grace, rather than enjoy the freedom in Christ that brings us closer to God and helps us become more like Jesus.

Paul warns us of the dangers of legalism. He admonishes us not to allow the shadows of things to distract us from engagement with the substance of things.

To judge one another concerning shadows is to waste our time and attention on the distorted images of real things.

We may miss the true light; the concrete reality Christ offers us if we entangle ourselves in the dark, insubstantial world of shadows.

Jesus is the sole source of all rule and authority.

There is no rule or authority apart from Him.

We know from the scriptures that God gets His way in Heaven. He doesn't always get His way on earth. God wants us to pray that He gets His way on earth. We would all be much better off if He did.

All authority flows from Christ, but that does not mean they obey Christ. We need only open our eyes to know this is so.

IMITATIONS AND EAR-TICKLERSrs

Colossians 2:18 Let no one keep defrauding you of your prize by delighting in self-abasement and the worship of the angels, taking his stand on visions he has seen, inflated without cause by his fleshly mind.

Paul warns us we should not let people who boast about how spiritual they are cheat us of our reward.

He mentions three ways false teachers deceive the gullible and immature:

- They abuse their bodies.
- They brag about their encounters with angels.
- They base their "ministries" on visions they claim to have received.

The common element? False leaders make themselves, not God, the center of attention.

Their message?

"I am more important, more spiritual, more mature than you because I have had these experiences, and you have not."

They cover their pride with a thin patina of false humility.

Too many biblically-illiterate Christians are led astray by such people when they chase after excitement instead of walking in genuine love and truth.

False leaders cause damage with their religious dog-and-pony shows and ear-tickling teaching.

We ought to avoid them. Accept no substitutes.

There is a vast difference between sharing our testimonies concerning what the Lord has done for or through us, things that may include signs, wonders, and miracles, and making ourselves the central figure in a religious circus.

The first draws the listeners' attention to Jesus; the second glorifies the person telling the tale.

While we may sometimes be led by the Spirit to fast or otherwise deny the demands of the flesh, to boast about it is an act of pride. Fasting is supposed to be a private act of humility.

It is the same with angels. God's angels do not want worship or any other attention. They are ministering spirits, beings whose delight is to help carry out the plan of God.

Demons crave attention and worship just as much as their master, Satan, does. Let us rejoice that God's angels are faithful and victorious, and fallen angels are engaged in a lost cause.

There are many religions in the world founded on visions supposed to have been received by their founders.

Not all visions are from God. If a vision contradicts the scriptures, then it is a counterfeit. Reject it.

> *Revelation 12:11a And they overcame him by the blood of the Lamb and by the word of their testimony.*

When we share our testimonies, we may speak of times the Holy Spirit led us to fast and pray, visions we may have received, or of our encounters with angels.

Let us remember to maintain humility in the telling and exercise wisdom concerning when and with whom we share such things. Our testimonies ought not to glorify ourselves, but the Lord Jesus Christ.

God uses our personal stories to edify and encourage the Body and gather in His lost sheep. Thanks to the shed blood of Jesus, we have overcome the enemy.

CLING TO THE SOURCE

Traditional: *Colossians 2:19 And not holding fast to the **head**, from whom the entire body, being supplied and held together by the joints and ligaments, grows with a growth which is from God.*

Revised: *And not holding (fast to) the **source**, from whom the whole body receives nourishment and, held together by the joints and ligaments, grows with a growth which is from God.*

We sometimes wander away from genuine faith in Christ. When we do, we stop growing in the Lord.

We stop growing and begin to wither on the vine when we follow self-appointed, self-centered, attention-craving "ministers." They complicate the gospel, cluttering it with extra-biblical laws and requirements.

False leaders misuse God's resources and suck the life out of us.

If we follow them, we trade living bread for dried crusts, and living water for stagnant slime.

We have let go of the joints and ligaments that join us to Christ; we have taken a path that leads us away from real faith.

Cut off from the flow of genuine living water, we not only cease to grow; we begin to wither.

> *Proverbs 14:12 There is a way which seems right to a man, but in the end, it leads to death.*

Not to live in Jesus, our source, is to live in a desert far from the flow of living water.

Our judgment and opinions always seem right to us. If we are in Christ, the Holy Spirit, our counselor, can correct us.

If we do not belong to Christ, we do not have the Holy Spirit. Uncorrected, our judgment and opinions will lead us astray, even to the point of death.

Trapped in slavery to sin, we miss true freedom, found only in Christ.

Our feelings, thoughts, and actions, clouded by sin, may seem right to us; but if we reject the love and mercy of Jesus Christ, the path we have chosen leads us to death.

CLOSING THOUGHTS

I am fully convinced the scriptures are 100% accurate and reliable in their original languages, as given to us by a perfect and loving God.

I am just as sure the imperfect human beings who translated them from the original languages didn't always get it right.

Even though the Holy Spirit always gets it right, we do not always accurately hear what the Spirit says.

> *1st Corinthians13:12 For now, we see in a mirror dimly, but then face to face; now I know in part, but then I will know fully, just as I also have been fully known.*

Since the first translation of the Bible into English until today, translators have not always been able to avoid bringing their cultural pre-conceptions to their understanding of the scriptures.

While we ought to be concerned there are a few errors in English language translations of the Bible, we ought, even more, to rejoice there are so few!

We can take comfort that down through the ages, the translators mostly got it right!

I have done my best to ensure the accuracy of what I have written.

This study is the result of decades of prayer, research, and practical, grass-roots ministry among inmates, drug addicts, "normal" middle-class Christians, and church leaders.

I learned long ago no one who ministers in the name of the Lord Jesus Christ can afford to have an opinion concerning the meaning of the scriptures.

We cannot rely on the opinions of others; we must study them ourselves, especially if God has given us a public platform and the opportunity to influence thousands, even millions of people.

Thank you for taking the time to read this book. I pray the Lord Jesus Christ, by the power of the Holy Spirit, will empower you for many works of service.

May you find joy in the exercise of your God-given gifts for the glory of the Lord and the edification and comfort of humankind.

ABOUT THE AUTHOR

Bishop Richard H. and Reverend Dawn Marie Johnson have been engaged in full-time ministry throughout the United States and Canada since 1994.

For almost ten of those years, Richard, Dawn, and their kids lived full-time in a fifth-wheel trailer in church parking lots all over North America.

They had ministered in thirty-eight states and four Canadian provinces by the time they came off the road in 2005.

They led thousands of people to the Lord. They brought comfort and encouragement to hurting people in prisons, jails, juvenile detention centers, residential reentry programs, churches, home fellowships, and many other venues.

In January of 2005, Richard and Dawn started *Christian Formation Ministries, Inc. (CFM)* in New Albany, Indiana. Their volunteers and Community Chaplains minister to inmates, addicts, their children, and their immediate families, both inside and outside prison.

Married in 1985, Richard and Dawn have two grown children; Rev. Suzanna Jacobson and Jimmy Johnson, and three (so far) grandchildren.

Suzanna took over the leadership of CFM in 2015. She is a gifted leader and motivator. Jimmy quietly ministers to young people involved in the online international gaming community. He manages a tabletop gaming store in Louisville, Kentucky.

Bishop Richard is a husband, father, grandfather, teacher, writer, and musicianary, a purveyor of "Christian swamp music," with numerous recordings to his credit. He was known for years as "Stonefingers" except in Arkansas, where they just called him "Stone."

Richard was ordained a Minister of the Gospel in 1995 and commissioned a Bishop and Apostle in 2017.

He did such an excellent job during his years as a Prison Chaplain that they shut down the facility where he served.

Richard is involved in the *My Recovery Community* and other aspects of CFM's ministry;

He also mentors church and parachurch ministry leaders. He continues to write books, music, life skills curricula, ministry training materials, resources for recovery and reentry, and scripture commentaries.

Reverend Dawn is a fifth-generation minister and a gifted teacher, preacher, and exhorter. You might say it's in her blood. She was ordained a Minister of the Gospel in 2000.

Dawn is a wife, mother, grandmother, and the co-founder of Christian Formation Ministries. She has also enjoyed success in the business world as a trainer, curriculum writer, and IT specialist. Her business-related skills are extremely useful in ministry.

She is CFM's Volunteer and Chaplaincy Training Director and develops many of our unique ministry resources.

An experienced prison minister and mentor, Dawn has tremendous discernment and is gifted by God to facilitate the healing of past emotional traumas and the pain they cause.